OCTAVE

and his

PIANO

**Written and illustrated by
Gérard Moncomble**

**Assisted by
Bruno Vincent**

To my little musicians

FINDING OUT ABOUT INSTRUMENTS

foulsham educational

To Philippe Blacher, Jaqueline Lasvènnes
and Bernard Labedade;
to Serge Carrère, Michel Trublin
and to Bruno Vincent whose idea this book was,
a fully orchestrated thank you.

Gérard Moncomble

Design (Cover and Contents):
Jean-Louis COUTURIER
Lay out: Monique DIDIER

Printed in Czechoslovakia.

ISBN 0-572-01966-1

This anglicised edition copyright © 1994 W. Foulsham & Co. Ltd.
Original copyright © Bordas, Paris

foulsham
Yeovil Road, Slough, Berkshire SL1 4JH

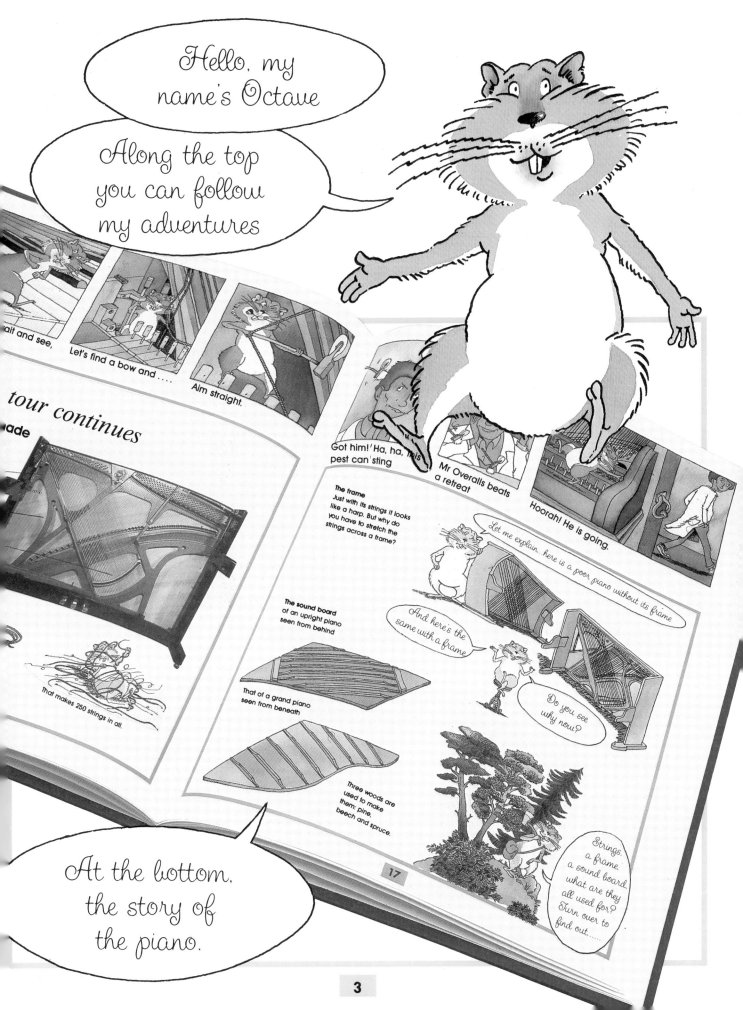

Hello, my name's Octave

Along the top you can follow my adventures

At the bottom, the story of the piano.

ait and see.

Let's find a bow and . . . .

Aim straight.

Got him!' Ha, ha, this pest can sting

Mr Overalls beats a retreat

Hoorah! He is going.

tour continues

ade

That makes 250 strings in all.

The frame
Just with its strings it looks like a harp. But why do you have to stretch the strings across a frame?

The sound board
of an upright piano seen from behind

That of a grand piano seen from beneath

Three woods are used to make them: pine, beech and spruce.

Let me explain.. here is a poor piano without its frame

And here's the same with a frame

Do you see why now?

Strings, a frame, a sound board, what are they all used for? Turn over to find out......

17

Everybody has a home.

And this is mine.

*I*dentity

Cut!
Just as in cinema(tography),
or photo(graph),
the pianoforte
has lost a bit of
its name on the way.
Guess which bit.

Careful now! There are pianos and pianos

The grand piano

Distinguishing marks:	shaped like the wing of a plane because its strings lie horizontally.
Date of birth:	between 1710 and 1720.
Place of birth:	Italy, France, Germany.
Width:	1.50 metres.
Height:	between 0.95 and 1 metre.
Depth:	from 1.35 metres (baby) to 2.90 metres (concert).
Weight:	between 250 and 850 kilograms.
Basic materials:	wood, cast iron, ivory, wool felt, steel, copper.

This morning, as usual
I had my little swing.

my round of golf...

and my little
jog on the terrace.

**One is lying down,
one is standing up.**
The grand piano needs
a lot of room. It is
at its best in concert
halls.
The smaller upright piano
can fit in anywhere.
In your own room,
for example.

Right. Before we go on, do you have your passport with you?

The upright

Distinguishing marks:	the strings lie vertically.
Date of birth:	between 1800 and 1830.
Place of birth:	France, England.
Width:	between 1.43 and 1.58 metres.
Height:	between 1 and 1.03 metres.
Depth:	0.55 metres.
Weight:	between 140 and 240 kilograms.
Basic materials:	wood, cast iron, ivory, wool felt, steel, copper.

I was just about to have a nap in my hammock,

when, suddenly, a gang of robbers burst into the attic!

A piano is

cumbersome

heavy

Octave!

fragile

And my whole house was off down the stairs,

the doors locked behind it,

and off we went. Where on earth are these two bandits taking me?

. . . but it is not

a musical box
which plays by itself

Cheers everyone!

a drinks cupboard

an exotic bird
in a cage

Black and white
*On my lyre,
with its pedals
up and down,
I pad like a wolf,
gallop like a horse,
sometimes black, sometimes white,
with a wing and three feet.
Who knows
who I am?
I know, says a hand
At my touch you sing and sing
You're my friend, the piano!*

Everything's shaking, crashing, banging. We are having an earthquake!

When it was quiet, I stole a look outside.

I couldn't believe it!

*F*amily album

The piano has cousins everywhere among the keyboard, string and percussion instruments. Some may have a different shape and sound but they are very similar.

The harpsichord
Shaped like a piano but with two keyboards. The strings are plucked with quills.
Wings and quills, sounds like a bird!

Father Xylophone of the Keyboard Family

Eeer...

The spinet
Like the harpsichord but smaller: it needs less room because its strings run parallel to the keyboard. It looks like a large box in the shape of a butterfly.

My house was surrounded with masses of others. Small ones, big ones, white ones, black ones. A whole village!

The cymbalom
You might think this was a table but it's played on with hammers not knives and forks!

The celesta
It gives out a sound like bells ringing, but you play it with your fingers.

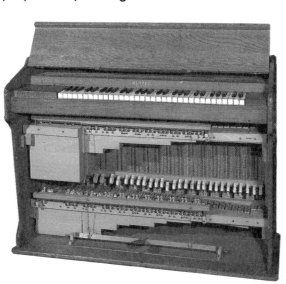

This is my new invention! The longest piano in the world for the energetic ones.

I must have some neighbours now.

Perhaps they are all in here, judging by the number of chimney pots.

I knew there was someone here.

*F*amily album continued

The synthesizer
Electronic, so it can imitate any instrument and also create its own sounds

The xylophone
Made out of wood, just like Pinocchio. You strike the keys with two sticks.

"Quiet! Do you want to wake up Mr Overalls?"

"He is huge! Terrifying! A monster!"

"And the row he makes repairing our houses!"

"Let's get out of his way!"

The accordion
Sometimes known as the piano with braces. It breathes in and blows out and everyone gets dancing.

The organ
Several keyboards for your hands and another for your feet. And then, wind in the pipes to make them sound like gigantic flutes.

And what about my fantastic family?...

"He's been after us for years."

"My grandfather told me so."

"Yes, and my grandfather's father said so too . . . "

Where does the piano come from?

It is not a very old instrument, but the idea behind it, that of tapping on a string, has been around for a long time. Maybe it all started when somebody struck the string of a psaltery instead of plucking it.

Dulcimers, timpans, clavichords, pianofortes. . . Over the years, each intrument has introduced a new element, but they all get on well together. It was the piano, however, that gradually established itself as the king of the keyboard instruments.

It has changed since 1700. Not in its shape, which is still very much like the harpsichord, but in its mechanism, which has become more and more precise.

The psaltery
An ancient instrument. The strings are either stroked with the fingers or plucked with quills.

The Timpan
One of the harp family. You strike the strings with curved sticks. It is the forerunner of the cymbalom.

"I'm afraid of nothing"

"Absolutely nothing."

"Now look what you've done. He's coming! "

The pianoforte

1703: bang! Bartolomeo Cristofori had the idea of striking strings with hammers, instead of plucking them like the harpsichord. So you could then play softly (piano), or loudly (forte). Hooray!

The clavichord

A sort of psaltery with a keyboard and a case. At the extremity of the keys are wooden or metal tangents which make the strings vibrate. It dates from the 12th century.

The pyramid piano

To make it easier to move, the wing was pushed upwards, like the modern upright. But it took on several shapes before assuming the one we know today: the lyre, the box and even the giraffe shape.

A giraffe piano? What about a hamster piano?

Mr Overalls!

Gracious me! He's taking my house to bits,

taking down my hammock.

Guided tour of the piano

The mechanism and the keyboard.
An amazing machine, an extension of the pianist's ten fingers.

For me its mechanism is just like a car engine

"Why are you breaking up my house?"

"Get out of here, you clumsy brute!"

"Clear off, you little pest!"

Riddle

Who has hammers, rods and bars, screws and tacks?

A carpenter.

No. It has also got heels and hammer heads and it is knobbly and wriggly.

A monster with chicken-pox.

No, you've lost.

It's neither, its the mechanism of a piano.

A keyboard with 88 keys

The black notes are made out of ebony.

The white ones used to be covered in ivory.

Today most of them have a plastic finish.

Me, a pest? You just wait and see, Mr Overalls!

Let's find a bow and . . . .

Aim straight.

The tour continues

How the sound is made

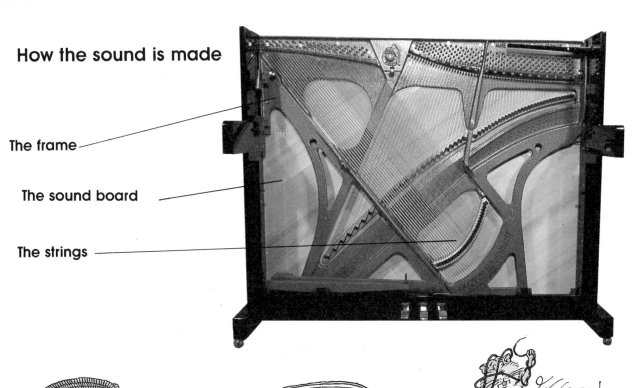

The frame

The sound board

The strings

The heavy strings
They are made of steel, covered in copper.

The light strings
They are made of steel.

That makes 250 strings in all.

Got him! Ha, ha, this pest can sting.

Mr Overalls beats a retreat.

Hoorah! He is going.

The frame
Just with its strings it looks like a harp. But why do you have to stretch the strings across a frame?

Let me explain ...here is a poor piano without its frame

And here's the same with a frame

Do you see why now?

The sound board
of an upright piano seen from behind

That of a grand piano seen from beneath

Three woods are used to make them: pine, beech and spruce.

Strings. a frame. a sound board. what are they all used for? Turn over to find out......

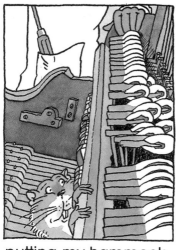

Even better, he's rebuilding my terrace,

putting my hammock back

and tightening up my swing ropes.

The strings vibrate. . .

When a string vibrates, it produces a sound.

The sound is low

The sound is high

if the string is slack

if the string is pulled tight

if it is thick

if it is thin

if it is long

if it is short

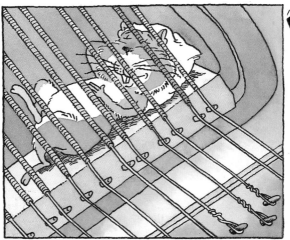

At last! Now for a bit of peace . . .

Suddenly, I was shaken to bits.

Oow, what's that ghastly row?

. . . and the sound board amplifies the vibrations

just as a cave amplifies your voice

ten green bottles

Wait for the bang!

With no sound board

With a sound board

The piano has a lid
If you lift it up, you can increase the sound or send it in a certain direction

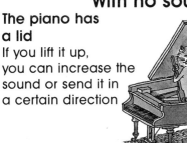

HEY, NOT THIS WAY!

Upstairs, my golf clubs sound more like pneumatic drills.

I can't get out of their way.

Quick. I've got to find a way out of this mad house!

*H*ow does the piano work?

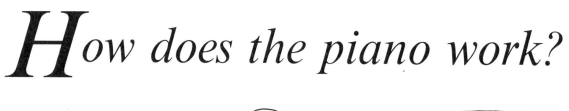

And there's old man Overalls thumping away on my terrace.

"This is my house! I want some peace"

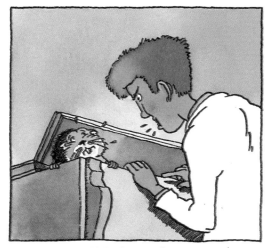

"What? But this is a piano and I'm playing music on it!"

Octave has fallen onto the pedals
The left one is the soft pedal. The middle one mutes the sound. The one on the right is the loud pedal.

Help! I'm slipping!

That's the last time I'll play the fool

Between you and me, and speaking as a pianist, I would not recommend a swimming costume. However, my advice is to use your hands. Much better for piano playing.

Piano? Music? What is he on about?

You are not a house-repairer, then?

"No, I'm the piano man. I take it to bits, clean it and adjust it."

*W*ho does what in the making and mending of a piano?

The wood
After the wood is cut, it is dried nice and flat, and out of the sun and rain, for years. It takes time for wood to become a sound board:

Lots of helpers
The piano manufacturer used to be able to make a piano all on his own. Nowadays the piano industry needs about ten different specialists. It has become real team work.

The cabinet maker
He makes and assembles all the wooden exterior of the piano.

And you are just a stowaway."

So my house is no longer my house?"

Mr Overalls had a think. "I've got an idea."

The string fitter
He fastens the 250 strings to steel pegs.

The adjuster
He has to adjust each piece of the keyboard and the mechanism, 3,000 of them!

The tuner
He needs a key to turn the pegs and stretch the strings, and a tuning fork to give the A. Now the piano will sing in tune and it is your turn to play it.

But it's me who keeps things moving of course . . .

"A super idea! Want to know what it is?"

I'll be a concert mechanic.

But, board and lodging go with the job, mind.

*T*he Piano can be seen everywhere

On its own for the soloist's recital

For chamber music, with a few friends

When the pianist plays,

I'll be his right hand.

A broken string? I can mend it.

Two pianos together.
A back-to-back.

What a busy fellow!
Wherever there is music, there he is! You see, our piano can do everything: have a loud voice (the bass notes) or a tiny little voice (the high notes) and lots of others. In fact thanks to the wide spread of his notes he could play the scores of an entire symphony orchestra. As he can play both the tune and the accompaniment, he can interpret, all by himself, different sorts of compositions: sonatas, concertos, songs, fugues and fantasies, variations or rhapsodies and even Satie's "pear-shaped piece"!
I am sure you have not heard the last of him.

It's jazz time so he can go bananas

banana piano

panana biano eer...

panaba .....

gue up!

A hammer gets stuck. I'll unstick it!

A pedal's rubbing? I'll file it down!

A broken castor? I'll prop it up!

*E*verywhere...

It is the composer's work bench

It can discreetly accompany a song

Twenty fingers at the same time

Getting hot and sticky?
I'll mop his brow!

I am IN-DIS-PEN-SA-BLE

and so E-FFI-CIENT.

A symphony orchestra

Why don't we get them all on to a football pitch?

And if I have a free moment,

I'll tap out a tune on the top of my musical house,

or do some arabesques with a balle dancer in a tutu.

The pianist and his piano

"I decided I would be a musical instrument my whole life through. You can only play music with your heart. What you sing within will come to your fingertips unaided"

Arthur Rubenstein
(extract from the book Arthur Rubenstein ou l'amour de la vie, É. Lipmann, éd de Messine)

The soloist
A pianist is, above all, a soloist. With his ten fingers, two feet and eighty-eight black and white keys, he can play anything. And there are not many musicians who can be a one man band.

The hands
They don't have a moment's peace, flying up and down the keyboard. They are real athletes, stroking, attacking, striking and hammering.

The feet
They have to work hard too. As they press down on the pedals, they soften or amplify the sound.

The score
This is the written part of the music. Usually in a concert the pianist does not need it: he knows his music by heart. This enables him to interpret it as he wishes.

The music stand
The piano is one of the few instruments to have its own, very handy.

The piano stool
This is adjustable. But what do you do when your feet do not reach the pedals?

Tuning
Unlike most other musicians, the pianist does not tune his own instrument. When the pianist comes on to play, the tuner has already done his job and everything is ready. A piano has to be tuned before each concert.

The castors
These make you realise the piano is a very heavy instrument. You would need a very big suitcase to carry it in. This means that the concert pianist never plays his own piano. He discovers a new one each time and has to get used to it and get the feel of it.

She'd make a wonderful pianist!

The audience will love me   . . . and I them.

Even if it is a job that has its ups and downs.

See you again in my other books for more adventures....

PICTURE CREDITS

Photographs by Jean PORTES and Francoise VERGNES :
• **p. 4** : *Grand piano* • **p. 5** : *Upright piano* • **p. 10** : *Synthesizer : Xylophone* • **p. 11** : *The organ of the Abbey of Moissac* • **p. 14** : *Mechanism and the Keyboard* • **p. 16** : *How sound is made* • **p. 23** : *String fitter : Adjuster : Tuner.*
• **p. 3** : Ph. M. Didier/© Photeb • **p. 8** : *Harpsichord attributed to J. Resnois,* about 1780. Musée des Jacobins, Auch, Ph. J.-M. Labat/© Arch Photeb : *P. Denis's spinet,* 1672 Musée instrumental, Paris, Ph. Publimages/© Arch Photeb • **p. 9** :*Cymbalum,* Ensemble Intercontemporian, Paris, Ph. Jeanbor/© Photeb : *Celesta,* Parc du material musical, Paris, Ph. Jeanbor/© Photeb • **p. 11** : *Accordion,* Ph. Jeanbor/© Arch Photeb • **p. 12** : *Psaltery, Virgin with child (detail)* by T. Vanni, Musée de Louvre, Paris, Ph © Giraudon ; *Timpan,* a detail of a miniature of the breviary of King Rene II of Lorraine, Bibl. de l'Assenal, Paris, Ph © Bibl. Nat/Arch Photeb • **p. 13** : *Harpsichord,* Spain 16th Musée Instrumental, Paris, Ph © Publimages/Photeb : *Pyramid piano,* 19th Musée Instrumental, Paris, Ph. © Publimages/Photeb; *Pianoforte,* by P. Taskin 1788, Musée Instrumental, Paris, Ph © Publimages/Photeb • **p. 22** : *Cabinet maker,* Ph © D. Partes • **p. 24** : *The Beaux-Arts Trio,* 1986, Ph © Th. Martinot, *Maurizio Pollini,* Ph © Th. Martinot • **p. 25** : *Güher and Süher Pekinel,* Ph. © Werner Neumeister; *Herbie Hancock,* Ph. © F. Perol • **p. 26** : *G. Vichnievskaia with Rostropovitch at the piano,* Ph. © G. Neuvecelle; *M. Béroff and J. P. Collard,* Ph. ©G. Neuvecelle; *J. Zitterer; Joseph Haydn,* about 1795, Mussender Stadt, Vienne, Ph. © Bridgeman-Giraudon • **p. 27** :*V. Ovchinikov and the Royal Liverpool Philharmonic Orchestra ,* Ph. © Clive Barda.
English translation Moira Allouche with technical advice from Nicholas Burton-Page, Professor of Early Music at the National Conservatoire of the Region of Aubervilliers - La Courneuve.